THE LITTLE KLIMT

Catherine de Duve

In association with the Réunion des Musées Nationaux

VIENNA

Until 1918, Vienna was the metropolis of the Austro-Hungarian Empire. The emperor François-Joseph, Sissi's husband, rules over an empire of 17 countries. The city is enlarged to greet newcomers and a huge boulevard is built around the city: the Ring. Majestic buildings, theatres, operas, parliaments, museum, a university, private houses are erected. They are decorated in a historic style, as if they had been standing there forever. The columns, arcades, sculptures, paintings, remind us of Greek temples or mediaeval cathedrals…

1900

Vienna is the city of music. Mozart, Beethoven, Schubert, Brahms and Strauss lived there. One hails a coach to go to the opera of which Mahler is the director. Freud writes his *Interpretation of Dreams.* Yet while some are having fun in the Prater Parc, or waltzing on the lacquered parquets of the café-concert halls and balls, a threat hovers over the imperial city. Could it be a taste of jolly 'Apocalypse' then? Vienna mixing up elements of renewal and decay glitters but not for much longer.

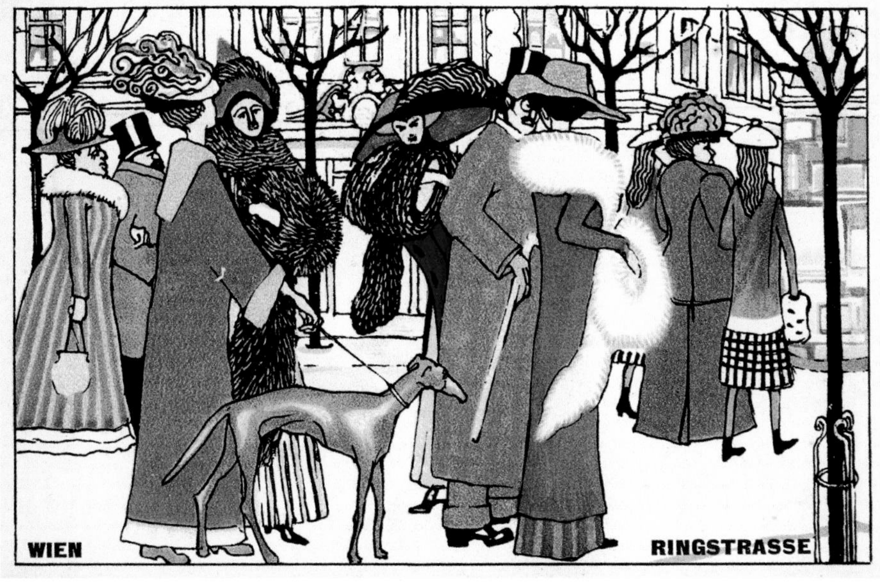

GUSTAV KLIMT

Gustav Klimt was born on July 4th 1862 in a suburb of Vienna. His father is a goldsmith; he chisels precious metals. Gustav has two brothers and four sisters, who shall be his first models. He studies at the Arts and vocational college in Vienna with his brother Ernst. Together with a friend they create an atelier: 'the Companionship of Painters' to decorate the walls and ceilings of palaces and theatres. The three young painters have a similar academic style. But what do they paint? Historic scenes, representing for example art history throughout times, from the Egyptian, Greek Antiquity to the Italian Renaissance as in the staircase of the Art history museum, at the Kunsthistorisches Museum.

Allegory of the Antique Gre

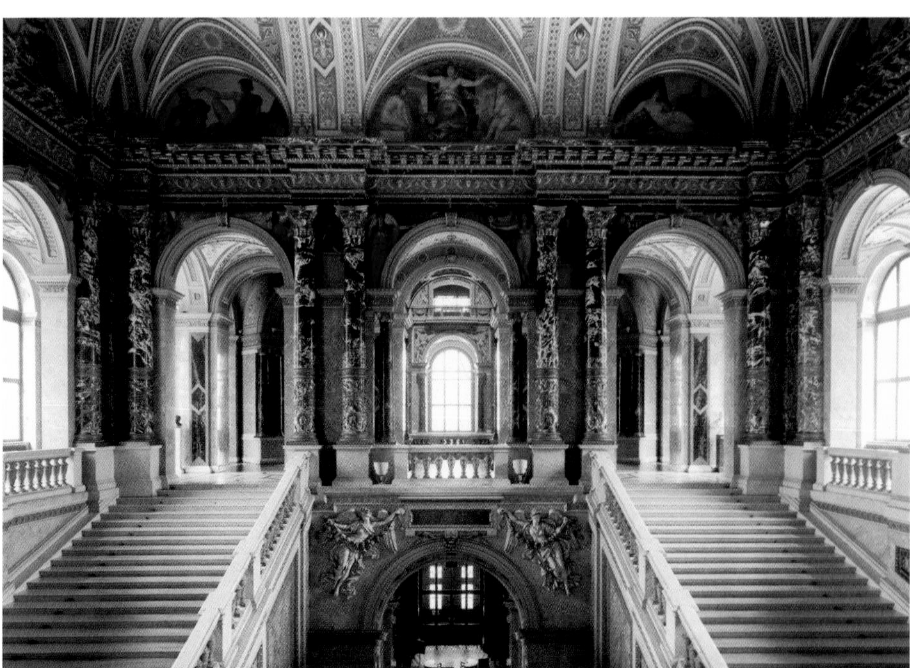

Yet little by little, Klimt detaches himself from the traditional style and paints in a more personal fashion. At his brother's death, the artist settles alone in an atelier. Klimt lives in an apartment with his mother and sisters. Often, early in the morning, he goes for a little walk before going to his atelier; he likes the little wild garden which surrounds it, the flowers and the many cats.

Look at Klimt in his atelier's garden.

VIENNESE SECESSION

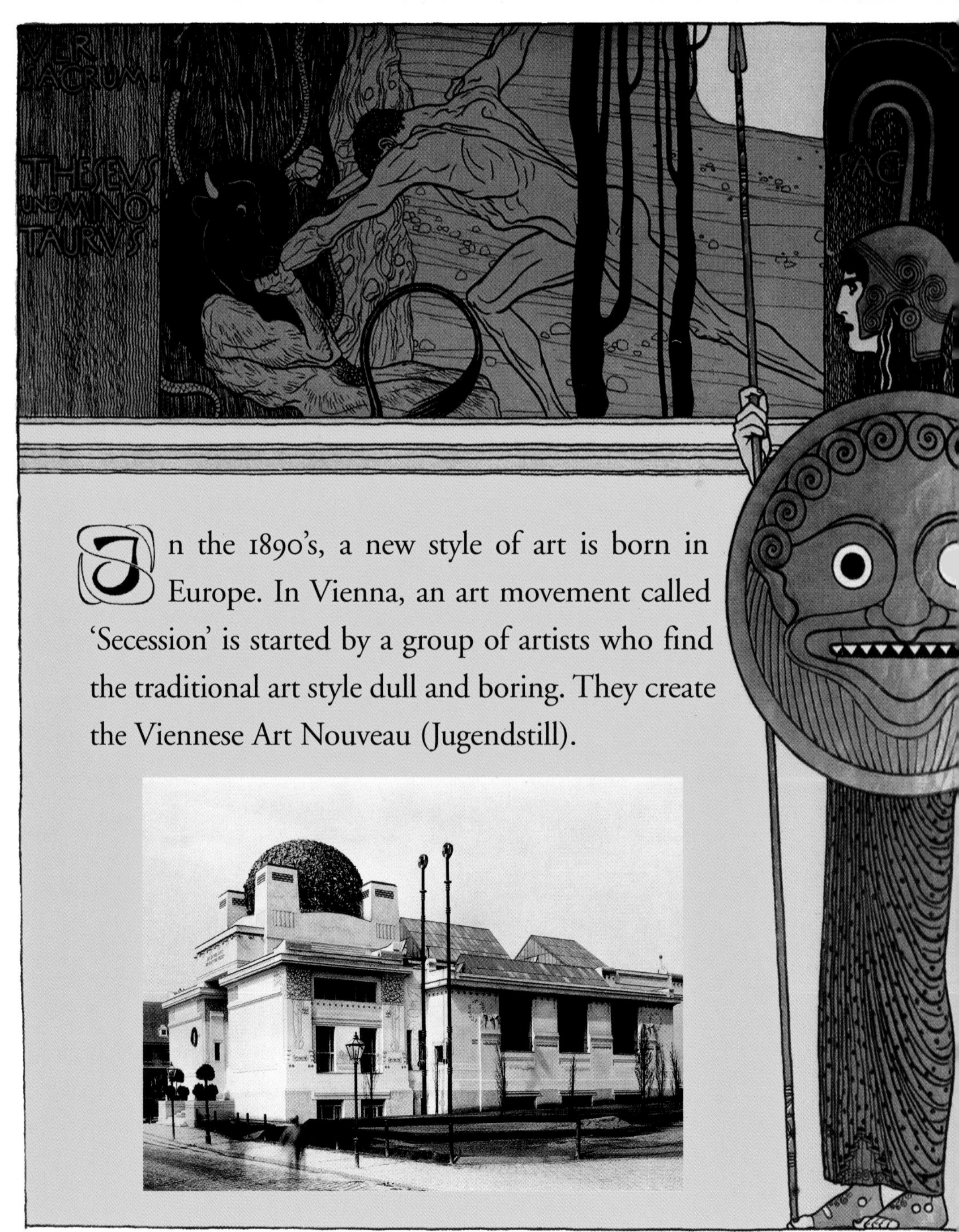

In the 1890's, a new style of art is born in Europe. In Vienna, an art movement called 'Secession' is started by a group of artists who find the traditional art style dull and boring. They create the Viennese Art Nouveau (Jugendstill).

In 1898 the Secession's exhibition pavilion opens its doors to the public. The architect Olbrich imagined new strait and geometrical shapes. It's a total work of art! Under its golden laurel dome, one reads 'to each period its art, to art its freedom'. But what does one do there? Novel artistic trends are exhibited, through the works of art of the member artists but also of guest artists from abroad, such as Rodin, Van Gogh, Khnopff, Signac… They publish a review entitled 'Ver Sacrum' to reach out to the general public. Art should be useful to all. Furniture, jewellery, clothes are created. In 1902, Klimt paints a 34m long narrow mural in the pavilion, called a frieze. He was inspired by Beethoven's *Ninth Symphony.*

Look at this detail of the frieze. What do you think the strange characters are doing?

GORGON

Wrapped in her golden scale breastplate, Pallas Athena, the Goddess of wisdom, war and arts, is staring at us. She holds a spear in one hand and a small figure in the other, a little woman representing the naked truth. It is an *allegory.* Klimt paints in his favourite format: the square. The frame is made in pushed timber by his brother, Georg.

Symbols of the goddess Athena are a helmet, spear, armour, owl and lyre. How many of them can you find in the painting?

What a horrible grimace! What sort of odd character is this one, pulling out his tongue at us? It is Medusa, one of the three gorgons. She has a woman's body and hair made of snakes. It is said that he who crosses her glance is turned into stone. Petrified in horror! Visitors coming to the second Secession Exhibition in 1898 were taken aback: 'What a face!', they thought. Are they frightened perhaps?

An ***allegory*** *is an idea represented by a character with objects or attributes of a symbolic nature. The lyre for example symbolises poetry, music and arts in general.*

Draw a Medusa making a face.

GOLDEN RAIN

It is said that the King of Argos had 50 daughters, called the Danaides. One of them, Danae, was locked up by her father in a tower to which no wooer had access. Yet Zeus, king of all gods, came to her. Disguised in thin droplets of golden rain, he slipped into the dark room. From their union was born a son, Persée. It is he who cut off the head of the Gorgon Medusa.

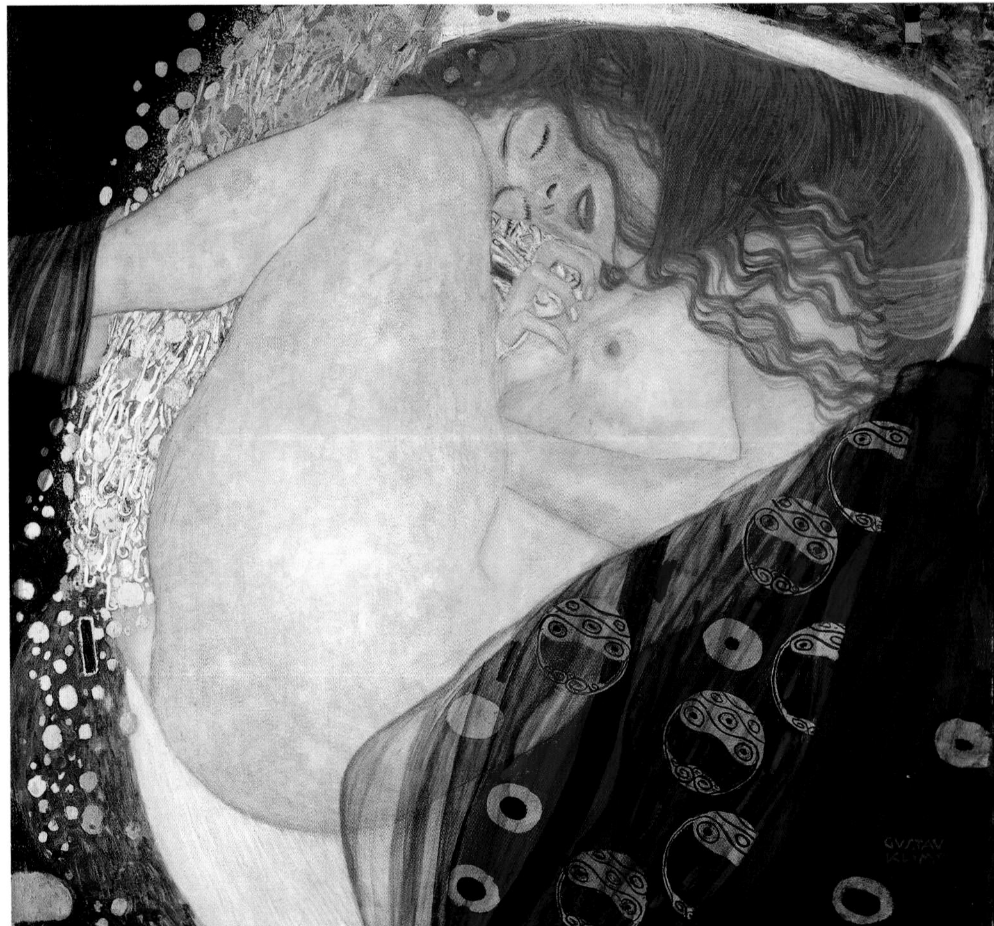

Klimt likes to paint women in private moments. Sometimes they are sleeping. Other times they look seductively at us. Klimt uses geometric shapes to shroud his paintings in mystery.

Observe the women painted by Klimt.

Hermine

Adèle

Fritza

Egyptian Lady

Salome

a mysterious woman

THE KISS

A tender stolen kiss. On a flying carpet, embroidered with multicoloured flowers a couple gently rests in each other's arms. The man is dressed with rectangular shapes and spirals while kissing the rosy cheek of a kneeling woman. Her dress is covered with round shapes and a little trail of golden triangles. Would Klimt be trying to represent eternal bliss?

Before making that painting around 1908, Klimt painted other kisses. Which one do you prefer?

ADORNMENT

In a golden imperial setting, the elegant Adèle poses on an imaginary throne. As an *icon,* she stares at us, while swimming in a bath of golden and silver embroideries. She wears sumptuous jewellery, bracelets and a choker. The artist has attached some precious metals to his canvas. Can you see them?

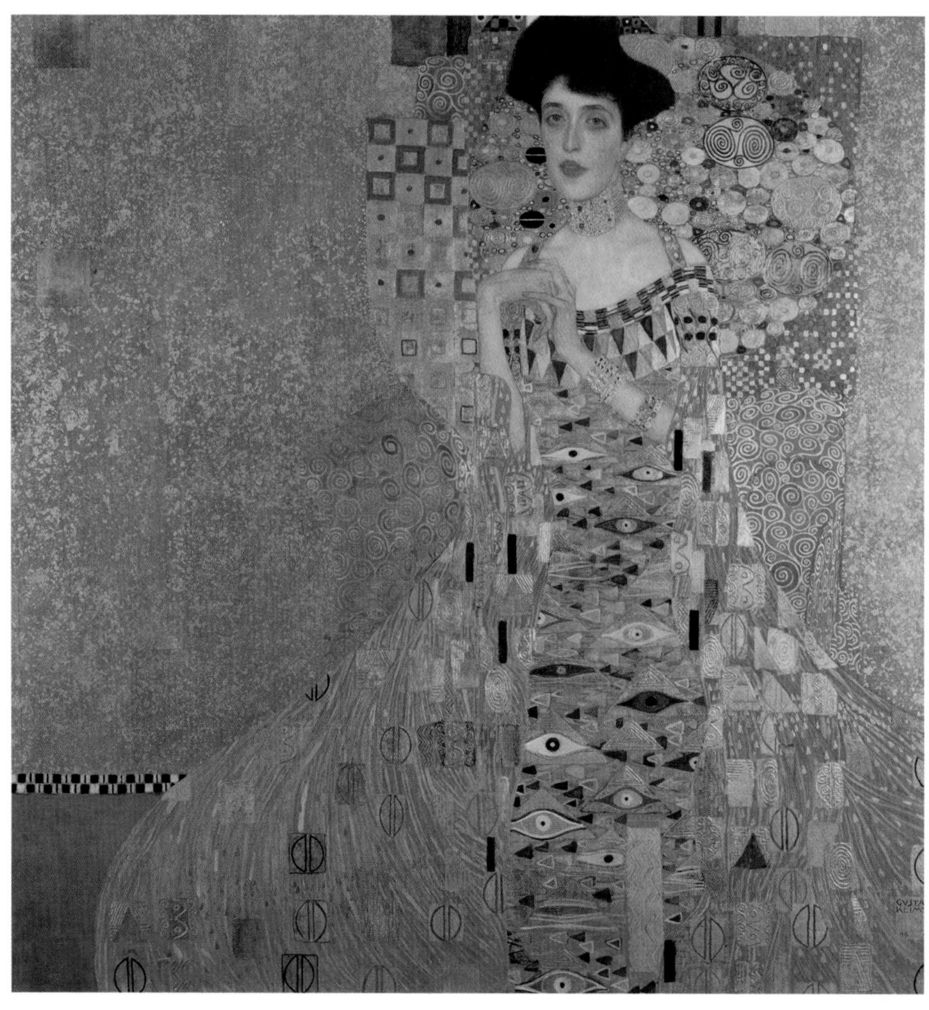

During a trip to Italy in 1903, Klimt discovers mosaics on a golden background in the churches of Ravenna. Back in his Viennese atelier, the artist imagines a luxurious and precious adornment. Again, Klimt draws his inspiration from geometrical shapes again. Squares, circles, triangles, ovals, spirals. Which ones do you spot?

In Russia, an ***icon*** *is a small wooden painting representing a sacred image. The background is often golden to reflect the divine element.*

Which of these patterns can you find in Adèle's portrait?

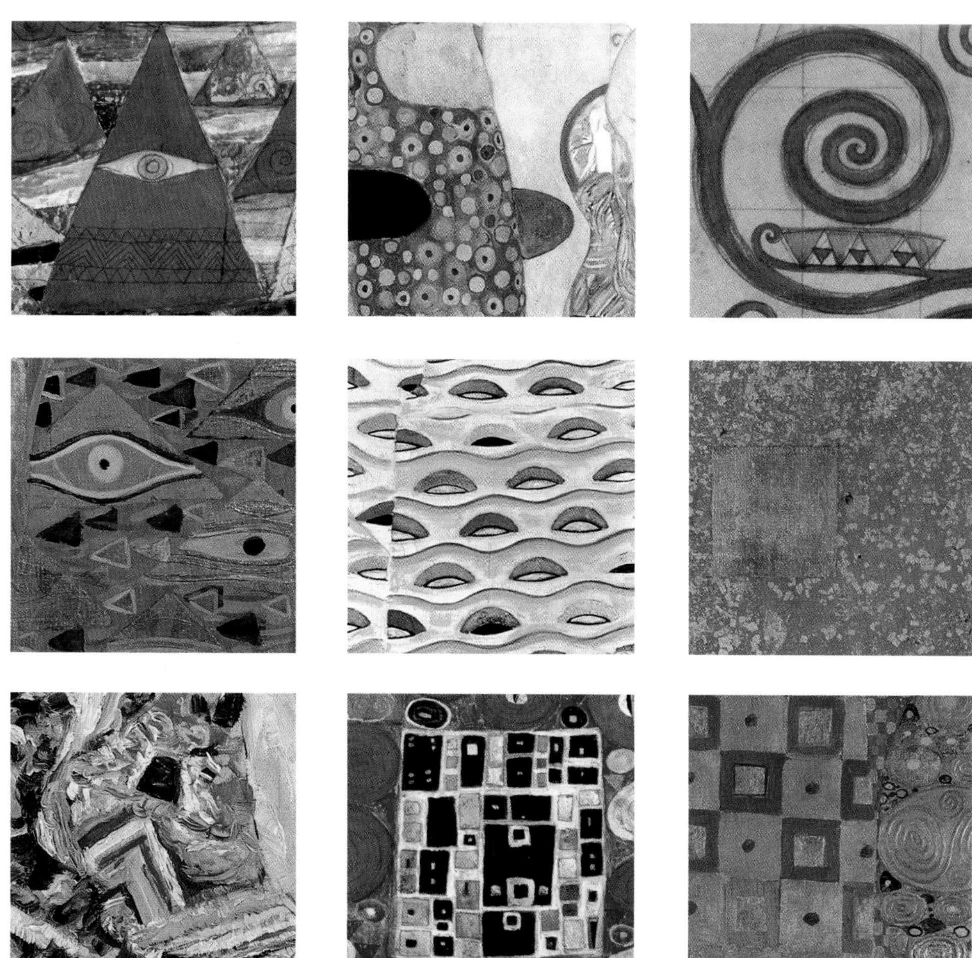

JEWEL

As an oriental dancer from an Egyptian painting, a woman glides to the left of the picture. She wears geometrical and golden pieces of jewellery on her arms and hair. Do you see eyes looking at her?

What lovely jewellery! Multicoloured bracelets with precious stones… And what a gaze! Would it be the legendary Judith or Salome? Both charmed a young man before having his head cut off for them! They are fatal women, beautiful and dangerous. Judith's hands are contracted as those of a witch and clamping at something. The young Viennese painters Egon Schiele and Oskar Kokoschka, both admirers of Klimt, also paint very expressive hands.

Make up your own design for a piece of jewellery.

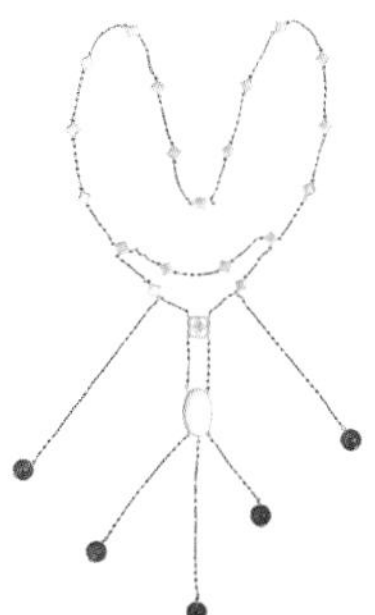

Jewellery drawn by Koloman Moser and offered by Klimt to Emilie Flöge.

Compare the hands painted by the three artists.

Klimt

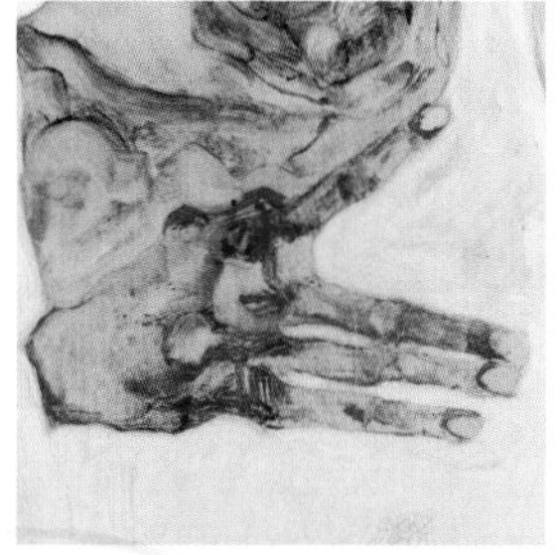

Schiele

Kokoschka

VIENNESE LADIES

Klimt is a painter at the top of the fashion. Rich Viennese ladies have their portraits made by him. Here is Hermine, the wife of an industrial business *mécène* of the Viennese Secession. She is wearing a white supple dress with a train, similar to those created by the avant-guard modellist 'Schwestern Flöge'.

A ***mécène*** *helps artists creating by buying their works of art.*

What do you think of Hermine's dress Does it look white or transparent? What kir of material is it?

Emilie Flöge.

The three Flöge sisters, Helen, Pauline, and Emilie, are famous for their corset free dresses. What a revolution! Thanks to this novel comfortable and light cut, women can finally regain a certain freedom of breath and no longer have to suffer in their strangulating corsets! Women gradually emancipate. They work, travel, dress more freely as Emilie Flöge does - Klimt's friend. Along with his friend Kolo Moser, Klimt creates some tunic models in the Viennese spirit, instituted by the Wiener Werkstätte since 1903. Geometric patterns, black and white stripes…

How many differences can you find between Emilie's dress and Hermine's? How are they similar?

HATS

'See how heavily made up this woman is! Blush on the cheeks, lipstick, fine eye shadow and mascara…' During the Belle Epoque, women would never think of going out without hat.

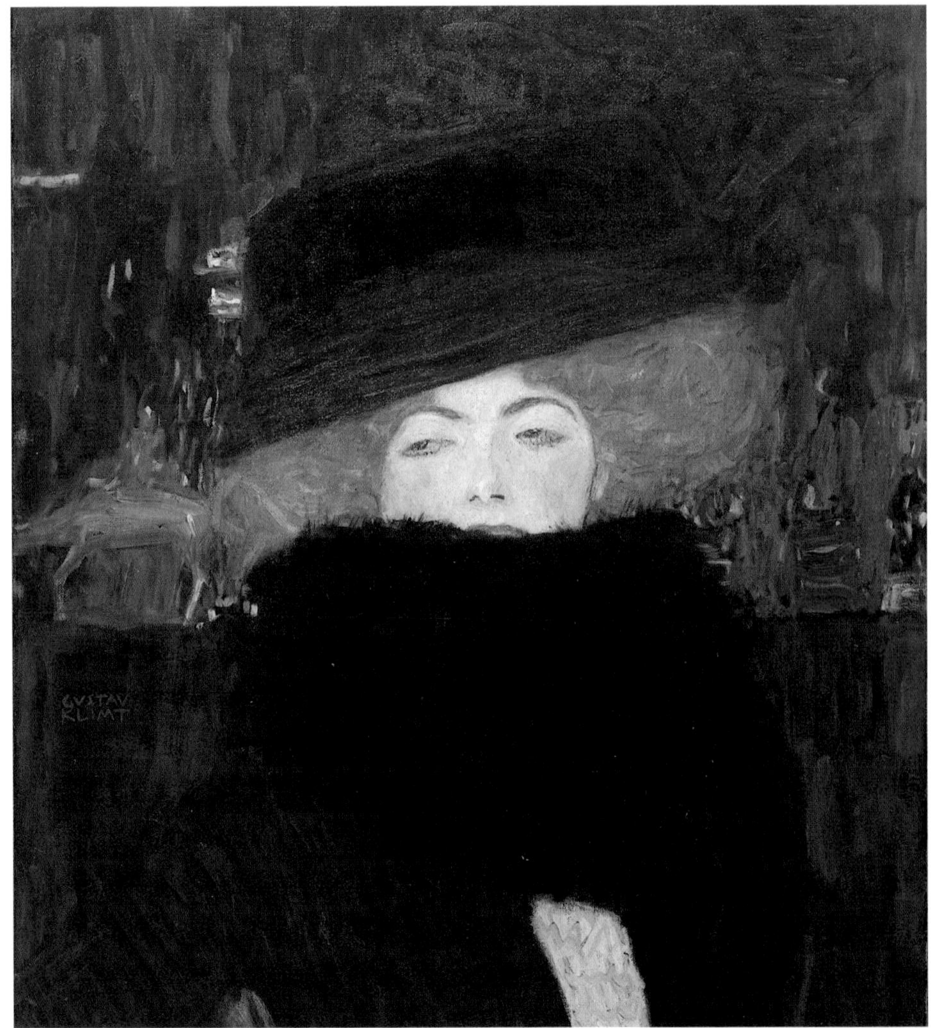

Toulouse-Lautrec.

Klimt paints women with a black feather boa or a large netted rim hat, in cabarets as the French painter Toulouse-Lautrec does. The Viennese painter has given up gold in all of his paintings and prefers more sober settings for them. What can you see in the background of Klimt's painting?

Feather hat or boa? Create your own fashion accessories.

"LA VIE EN ROSE"

How boring it is to pose for a painter! The little Mäda is 9 years old in the summer of 1912, when her mother brings her to Klimt's atelier. What self-confidence she radiates in her silk dress rimmed with roses! The wall is also covered with flowers and the carpet is woven with fantastic animals. Can you see them?

Find these details in the painting.

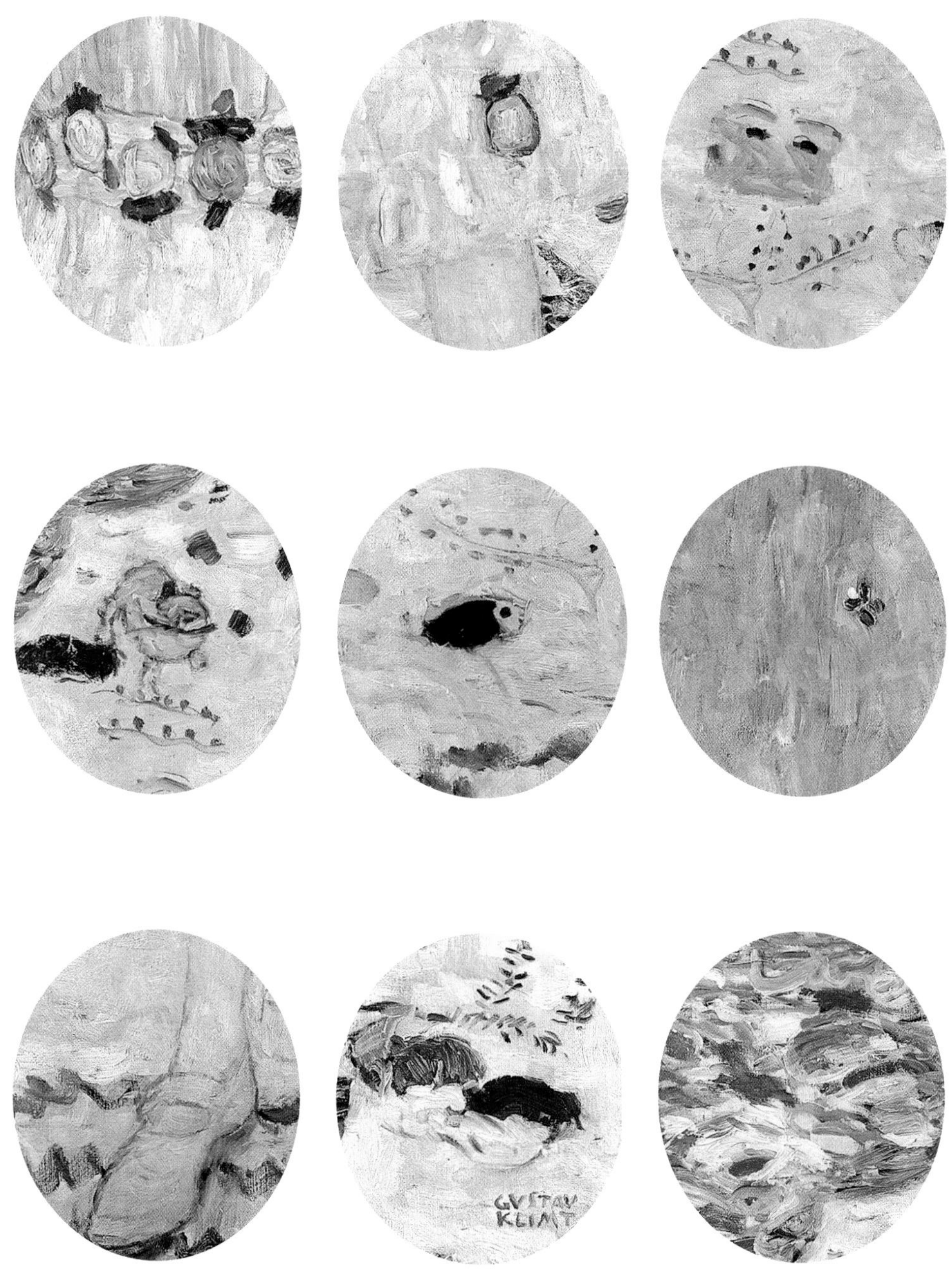

ORCHARD

Every summer, Klimt goes to the countryside to rest and paint landscapes. As the impressionist painters do, Gustav needs to brighten up his palette. He draws fruit trees in the orchard. But where is the line of horizon? Quite often, he creates his landscapes without perspective, as if he'd had his nose stuck on it. Don't these roses put on a human shape?

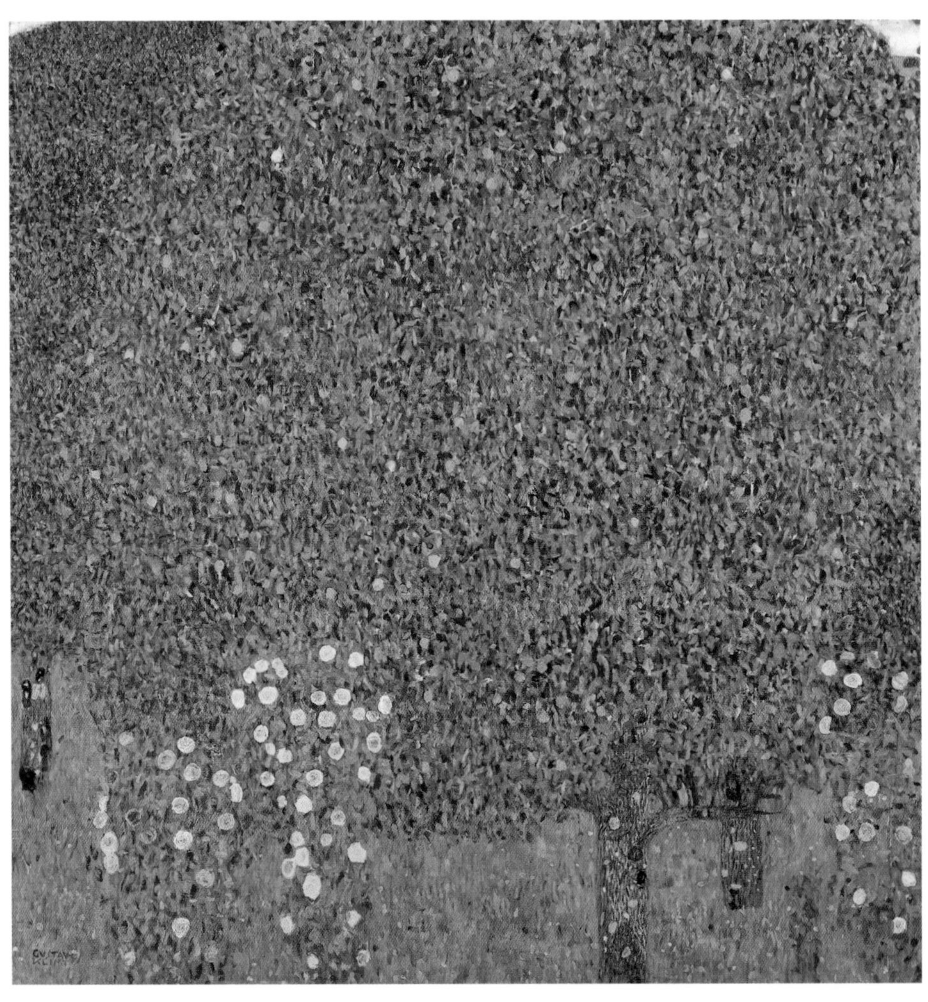

As many artists, Klimt likes to paint flowers.
Look at the three artists' style.

Monet Van Gogh Klimt

Find the details pertaining to the painting.

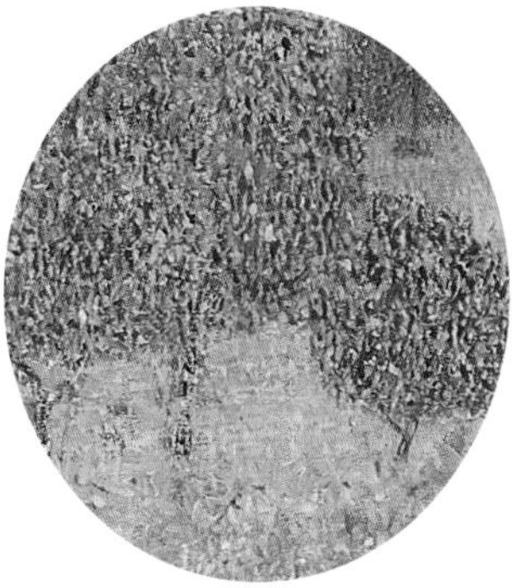

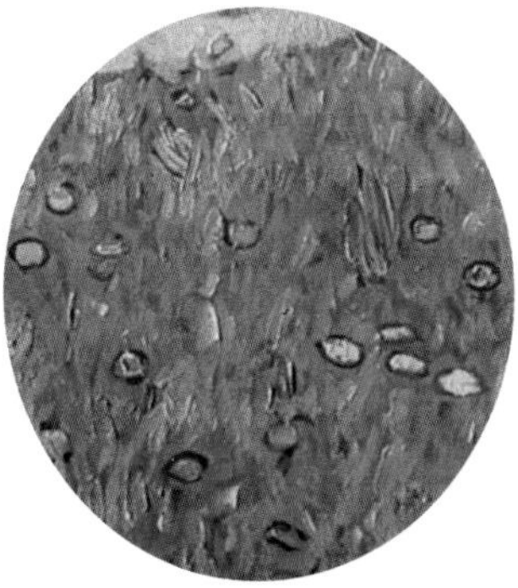

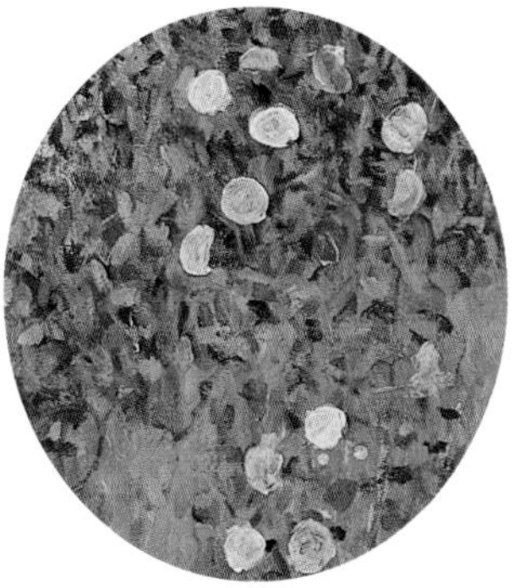

LAKE

Gustav and Emilie like to spend their summer holiday in the Highlands of Austria, on the banks of the Attersee, 250km from Vienna. Far from the city's tumult, the painter is happy and takes things easy. He brings his friend to sail out on the peaceful lake.

During the summer 1916, Gustav observes with a telephoto lens the other side of the lake, to paint the Unterach church. Strangely, everything appears different: it all seems flat. No clear pattern prevails over another.

Find the geometric shapes in the painting?

TREE

At the end of a shady road you can see the yellow façade of the Kammer castle, on the bank of the Attersee lake. The green and blue plane trees vibrate in the sun light. Leaves and branches are mingled. Klimt draws his inspiration from impressionist painters. Van Gogh's influence can be felt after Klimt attended an exhibition of his in 1906 in Vienna.

Suddenly, the sky darkens and the thunder rolls. Can you hear it? The leaves tremble with the wind, while the bark of the tall poplar is swaying. The artist chose to paint the leaves with small dots of colour in a pointillist style, as the skin of a 'tabby trout'. At the foot of the tall tree, wouldn't the little white chapel be a nice shelter?

Compare the different styles used in these two paintings.

BABY

A child fell asleep in the arms of his mother. Set aside on the left, an elder women hides her forehead in her hands. Is she crying? Around them, there is a curtain of dark and rainy shadows.

Assign an age to each character in the painting.

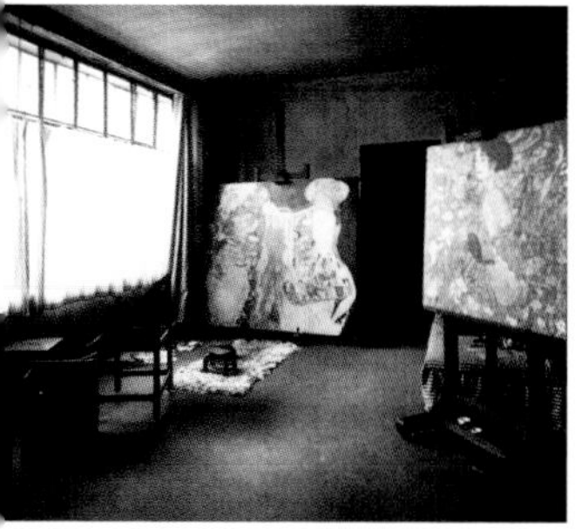

But soon, the doors of the artist's atelier close down for ever. Gustav Klimt dies in Vienna on February 6th 1918, at 55 years old. A few months later, the First World War ends and the Austro-Hungarian Empire collapses.

This is one of his last paintings. Who is hiding under all that stuff? The head surrounded by lace, a baby is babbling. Klimt's life was full of colours.

Text: Catherine de Duve
Graphic design: Philippe Plumhans
Concept and coordination: Kate'Art Editions & Happy Museum!
Translation: Alexa Parr & Wenda O'Reilly, Ph. D.

Photographic credits:

Gustav Klimt:

VIENNA: Österreichische Galerie Belevedere: *The Kiss,* 1907-08: cover page, p. 12, - *Portrait of Adèle Bloch-Bauer I,* 1907: pp. 11, 14-15 - *Portrait of Fritza Riedler,* 1906: pp. 11, 15 - *Avenue in the Park of Schloss Kammer,* 1912: p. 28 - *Lady with Hat and Feather Boa,* 1909: pp. 11, 20 - *Poppy Field*, 1907: p. 25 - *The Beethoven Freeze, "The Enemy Powers",* 1902: p. 7 & *"Joy, Nice and divine Sparkle",* 1902: p. 13 | **Wien Museum:** *Pallas Athene,* 1898: pp. 8-9 - *Theseus and the Minotaurus, poster for the first Secession exhibition,* 1897: p. 6 | **Leopold Museum-Privatstiftung:** *The Large Poplar II (Approaching Storm),* 1902-03: p. 29 - *On the Attersee,* 1901: p. 26 | **Österreichische Museum für Angewandte Kunst:** *The waiting,* work project for the *Stoclet Freeze,* around 1905-09: cover page, pp. 11, 15, 16-17 & *The Accomplishment,* work project for the *Stoclet Freeze,* around 1905-09: p. 13 | **Kunsthistorisches Museum:** *The Antique Greece,* 1890-01: p. 4 | **Hans Dichand Collections:** *Danae,* 1907: pp. 10,11 | **Private Collection:** *Church in Unterach on the Attersee,* 1916: p. 27 - *Forester's House in Weissenbach on the Attersee,* 1912: cover, p. 25

ZUG: Kunsthaus Zug., Stiftung Sammlung Kamm: *Garden Landscape with Hilltop,* 1916: p. 25

MUNICH: Neue Pinakothek, Bayerische Staatsgemäldesammlungen: *Music I,* 1895: p. 9

PARIS: Orsay Museum, RMN: *Roses under Trees,* around 1905: pp. 24, 25

ROME: National Gallery of Modern and Contemporary Art: *Three Ages of Woman,* 1905: pp. 1, 15, 30

VENICE: International Gallery of Modern Art Ca' Pesaro: *Judith II (Salome),* 1909: pp. 11, 17

LONDON: National Gallery: *Portrait of Hermine Gallia,* 1903-04: pp. 11, 18

WASHINGTON: Washington D.C., National Gallery of Art: *Baby (Cradle),* 1917: pp. 15, 31

NEW YORK: Metropolitan Museum of Art: *Portrait of Mäda Primavesi,* around 1912: cover, pp. 22-23

Réunion des Musées Nationaux: Claude Monet, *Poppies,* 1873: p. 25- **Henri de Toulouse-Lautrec,** *Jane Dancing April,* around 1892: p. 21
The Israel Museum: Vincent Van Gogh, *The Green spikes,* 1888: p. 25
Leopold Museum-Privatstiftung, Vienna: Egon Schiele, *Self-portrait with Black Clay Vase and Spread Fingers:* p. 17
Österreichische Galerie Belevedere, Vienna: Oskar Kokoschka, *Portrait of Carl Moll,* 1913: p. 17

Photographies and documents:

View on the Ring, Vienna around 1890: p. 2 - Imagno/Austrian Archives: *Ringstrasse, Vienna,* Jung Moriz, around 1912: p. 3 *& In the ball room,* M. Munck, around 1905: p. 3 - *Staircase of the Kunsthistorisches Museum:* p. 4 - *Klimt in front of his atelier in Josephstädtstrasse in Vienna with one of his cats in the arms. Photography by Moriz Nähr,* around 1912: p. 5 - *Klimt in the garden of his atelier:* p. 5 - *The Secession pavilion, soon after its construction:* p. 6 - *Necklace of Koloman Moser,* Fischer Fine Art (Emilie Flöge funds): p. 17 - *Sketch for the Sister Flöge company:* p. 18 - *Emilie Flöge wearing a strip and black and white square dress drawn by Klimt:* p. 19 - *Emilie Flöge, Photographie of Ora Banda, 1909.* Österreichische Nationalbibliothek, Vienna: p. 19 - *Gustav Klimt and Emilie Flöge in a boat on the Attersee lake,* vers 1910: p. 26 - Imagno/Austrian Archives: *Gustav Klimt looking through the looking glass at the Attersee lake,* 1904: p. 27 - *Photography of Klimt's atelier with the master's last painting, The Bride and the Lady with a fa, 13 Feldmühlgasse.* 1918: Klimt Archives, Albertina, Vienna: p. 31

With thanks to: Pierre Vallaud, Director RMN, Catherine Marquet, Director of RMN publications, Véronique Leleu, Jean-Baptiste Chantoiseau, Marie-Dominique de Teneuille, RMN publications, Dr Johanna Nestor, Dr Stephan Koja, Dr Franz Smola, Wenda O'Reilly, Ph. D., Daniel de Duve and everyone who helped to make this book.

www.happymuseum.com